ABRAHAM LINCOLN

THE LIBRARY OF CONGRESS

Pomegranate

SAN FRANCISCO

Pomegranate Communications, Inc.
Box 808022, Petaluma CA 94975
800-227-1428; www.pomegranate.com

Pomegranate Europe Ltd.
Unit 1, Heathcote Business Centre, Hurlbutt Road
Warwick, Warwickshire CV34 6TD, UK
[+44] 0 1926 430111; sales@pomeurope.co.uk

ISBN 978-0-7649-3768-2
Pomegranate Catalog No. AA351

Pomegranate publishes books of postcards on a wide range of subjects.
Please contact the publisher for more information.

Cover designed by Mariah Lander
Printed in China

19 18 17 16 15 14 13 12 11 10   11 10 9 8 7 6 5 4 3 2

To facilitate detachment of the postcards from this book, fold each card along its perforation line before tearing.

"I will make a prophecy that may now sound peculiar," abolitionist, diplomat, and Union officer Carl Schurz wrote to a friend October 12, 1864. "In fifty years Lincoln's name will be inscribed close to Washington's on this Republic's roll of honor." At the time it was written, Schurz's prophecy would have seemed far-fetched to many in the northern United States—quite probably including Abraham Lincoln. After three bloody years, the nation was still at war with itself, and the end was not yet in sight. Although William T. Sherman's Union armies were making some progress in the Western Theater (Atlanta had fallen September 2), the Union's powerful Eastern Theater force, the Army of the Potomac, which had suffered terrible losses during Ulysses S. Grant's Overland Campaign in the spring, was then engaged in a lengthening siege of Petersburg, Virginia. The incorporation of African American regiments into the Union army that had begun in late 1862 and the Emancipation Proclamation that Lincoln had issued January 1, 1863, remained ragingly controversial. A presidential election was looming, and it was by no means a foregone conclusion that Lincoln would win.

Today, we salute Schurz's prescience. The name of the sixteenth president of the United States is not only inscribed close to that of George Washington, first president and "father" of the nation; it often appears ahead of Washington's in scholarly and popular opinion polls of the nation's greatest chief executives. Lincoln's poetic eloquence, his grace under the most terrible pressures, his patience and firm persistence, his battles with melancholy, and his rippling good humor continue to inspire and fascinate the people of the United States and many others around the globe.

This book of postcards presents thirty images drawn from the collections of the Library of Congress, which include Lincoln's presidential papers and other Lincolniana, Civil War–era newspapers and other publications abounding in Lincoln stories and images, thousands of books about the sixteenth president, and many prints and photographs of Abraham Lincoln, from his days as a congressman to photographs taken just before his death.

—Margaret E. Wagner

TO ORDER REPRODUCTIONS OF IMAGES IN THIS POSTCARD BOOK: Note the Library of Congress negative number provided with the image (LC-USZ6-, USZ62-, or LC-B indicates b/w negative; LC-USZC4- indicates color transparency). Where no negative number exists, note the Library division and the title of the item. Duplicates may be ordered from the Library of Congress, Photoduplication Service, Washington, DC 20540-4570; phone: (202) 707-5640; fax: (202) 707-1771.

ABRAHAM LINCOLN

Abraham Lincoln, 1846 or 1847. Daguerreotype by Nicholas H. Shepherd.
Prints and Photographs Division, LC-USZC4-2439

BOX 808022   PETALUMA   CA 94975

Pomegranate

ABRAHAM LINCOLN

Abraham Lincoln, February 28, 1857. Photograph by Alexander Hesler.
Prints and Photographs Division, LC-USZ62-36582

BOX 808022 PETALUMA CA 94975

Pomegranate

ABRAHAM LINCOLN

Abraham Lincoln, two weeks before the final Lincoln-Douglas
debate in Pittsfield, Illinois, during Lincoln's unsuccessful bid for
the Senate. From an ambrotype by Calvin Jackson, October 1, 1858.
Prints and Photographs Division, LC-USZ62-16377

BOX 808022   PETALUMA   CA 94975

Pomegranate

For President

ABRAM LINCOLN.

For Vice President

HANNIBAL HAMLIN.

ABRAHAM LINCOLN

For President Abram Lincoln. Campaign banner for the 1860 presidential election. Color woodcut or lithograph by H. C. Howard, printed on muslin. Prints and Photographs Division, LC-USZC4-4616

BOX 808022   PETALUMA   CA 94975

Pomegranate

HARPER'S WEEKLY.

A JOURNAL OF CIVILIZATION.

Vol. IV.—No. 202.]

NEW YORK, SATURDAY, NOVEMBER 10, 1860.

[Price Five Cents.

Entered according to Act of Congress, in the Year 1860, by Harper & Brothers, in the Clerk's office of the District Court for the Southern District of New York.

HON. ABRAHAM LINCOLN, BORN IN KENTUCKY, FEBRUARY 12, 1809.—[Photographed by Brady.]

ABRAHAM LINCOLN

Hon. Abraham Lincoln, born in Kentucky, February 12, 1809. Wood
engraving on the cover of *Harper's Weekly,* November 10, 1860.
Prints and Photographs Division, LC-USZ62-122144

BOX 808022   PETALUMA   CA 94975

Pomegranate

ABRAHAM LINCOLN

Abraham Lincoln delivers his first inaugural address at the United
States Capitol, March 1861. Prints and Photographs Division,
LC-USZ62-48564

BOX 808022   PETALUMA   CA 94975

Pomegranate

ABRAHAM LINCOLN

Abraham Lincoln. Photograph included in an album collected by author and statesman John Hay, who was Lincoln's private secretary from 1860 to 1865. James Wadsworth Family Papers, Manuscript Division

BOX 808022   PETALUMA   CA 94975

Pomegranate

ABRAHAM LINCOLN

President Lincoln and His Cabinet, with Lieut. Genl. [Winfield] Scott.
(The unfinished Washington Monument is visible through the window.)
Lithograph by Kimmel & Forster, 1866. Prints and Photographs Division,
LC-USZ62-3559

BOX 808022   PETALUMA   CA 94975

Pomegranate

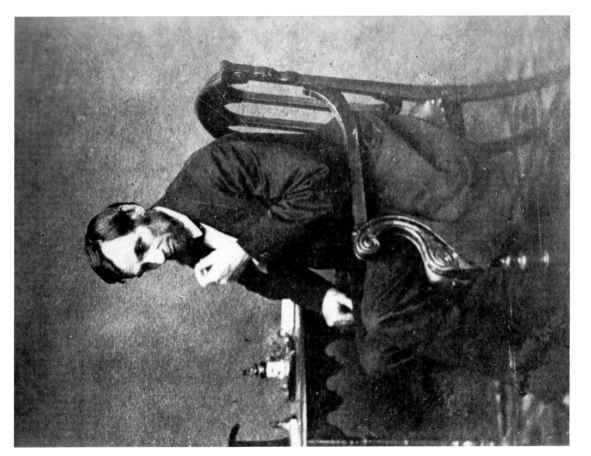

ABRAHAM LINCOLN

President Abraham Lincoln, 1862. Photograph by Mathew B. Brady.
Prints and Photographs Division, LC-USZ62-85666

BOX 808022   PETALUMA   CA 94975

Pomegranate

ABRAHAM LINCOLN

President Abraham Lincoln with General George B. McClellan and
other officers, Antietam, Maryland, October 3, 1862. Photograph by
Alexander Gardner. Prints and Photographs Division, LC-B8171-7951

BOX 808022   PETALUMA   CA 94975

Pomegranate

ABRAHAM LINCOLN

President Abraham Lincoln at Antietam, Maryland, October 3, 1862,
with Allan Pinkerton (left) and Major General John McClernand.
Photograph by Alexander Gardner. Prints and Photographs Division,
LC-B8171-7929

BOX 808022   PETALUMA   CA 94975

Pomegranate

ABRAHAM LINCOLN

President Abraham Lincoln and Major General George B. McClellan in
the general's tent at Antietam, Maryland, October 3, 1862. Photograph
by Alexander Gardner. Prints and Photographs Division LC-B8171-7948

BOX 808022 PETALUMA CA 94975

Pomegranate

ABRAHAM LINCOLN

Abraham Lincoln looking at an album with his son, Tad.
Photograph, between 1860 and 1865. Arthur Wallace Dunn Papers,
Prints and Photographs Division, LC-USZ62-92539

BOX 808022 PETALUMA CA 94975

Pomegranate

ABRAHAM LINCOLN

President Lincoln writing the Proclamation of Freedom, January 1st, 1863.
Color lithograph by Ehrgott, Forbriger & Co., 1864. Prints and Photographs
Division, LC-USZC4-1425

BOX 808022   PETALUMA   CA 94975

Pomegranate

ABRAHAM LINCOLN

Abraham Lincoln and His Emancipation Proclamation.
Color lithograph by the Strobridge Lith. Co., 1888.
Prints and Photographs Division, LC-USZC4-1526

BOX 808022   PETALUMA   CA 94975

Pomegranate

Executive Mansion.

Washington,   , 186

Four score and seven years ago our fathers brought
forth, upon this continent, a new nation, conceived
in liberty, and dedicated to the proposition that
"all men are created equal"

Now we are engaged in a great civil war, testing
whether that nation, or any nation so conceived,
and so dedicated, can long endure. We are met
on a great battle field of that war. We have
come to dedicate a portion of it, as a final rest-
ing place for those who died here, that the nation
might live. This we may, in all propriety do. But, in a
larger sense, we can not dedicate— we can not
consecrate— we can not hallow, this ground—
The brave men, living and dead, who struggled
here, have hallowed it, far above our poor power
to add or detract. The world will little note, nor long
remember what we say here; while it can never
forget what they did here.

It is rather for us, the living, to stand here,

ted to the great task remaining before us—
that, from these honored dead we take in-
creased devotion to that cause for which
they here gave the last full measure of devotion— that we here highly resolve these
dead shall not have died in vain; that
the nation, shall have a new birth of freedom, and that government of the people, by
the people for, the people, shall not per-
ish from the earth.

ABRAHAM LINCOLN

Abraham Lincoln's Gettysburg Address. Manuscript, 1863.
Manuscript Division

BOX 808022   PETALUMA   CA 94975

Pomegranate

ABRAHAM LINCOLN

President Abraham Lincoln, November 8, 1863. Photograph by
Alexander Gardner. Prints and Photographs Division, LC-USZ62-13016

BOX 808022   PETALUMA   CA 94975

Pomegranate

Abraham Lincoln

President Abraham Lincoln with his secretaries, John Hay and John
Nicolay. Photograph by Alexander Gardner, November 8, 1863.
Prints and Photographs Division, LC-USZ61-216

BOX 808022   PETALUMA   CA 94975

Pomegranate

Abraham Lincoln

President Abraham Lincoln, February 9, 1864. Photograph by Anthony
Berger of the Mathew Brady studio. Prints and Photographs Division,
LC-USZ62-15651

BOX 808022   PETALUMA   CA 94975

Pomegranate

GRAND, NATIONAL UNION BANNER FOR 1864.

LIBERTY., UNION AND VICTORY.

ABRAHAM LINCOLN

Grand National Union Banner for 1864. Liberty, Union and Victory.
Campaign banner for the 1864 presidential election. Lithograph
with watercolor on wove paper. Currier & Ives, 1864. Prints and
Photographs Division, LC-USZC2-2492

Pomegranate   BOX 808022   PETALUMA   CA 94975

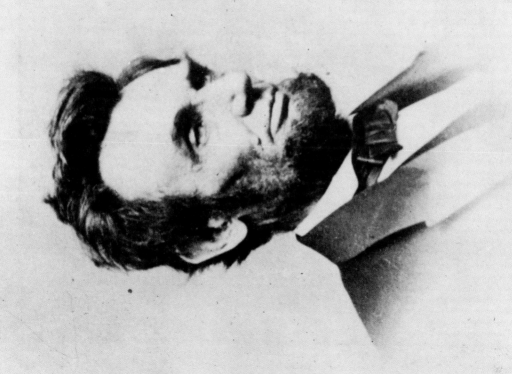

ABRAHAM LINCOLN

Abraham Lincoln. Photograph by Mathew B. Brady, 1864 (?).
Prints and Photographs Division, LC-USZ62-127571

BOX 808022   PETALUMA   CA 94975

Pomegranate

THE PIONEER BOY,

OR THE EARLY LIFE OF ABRAHAM LINCOLN.

12 MO. ILLUSTRATED. PRICE $1,50.

THE PRESIDENTS WORDS

A SELECTION FROM THE SPEECHES &c. OF

PRESIDENT LINCOLN.

EDITED BY EDWARD EVERETT HALE.

16 MO. PRICE $1,25.

SOLD BY ALL BOOKSELLERS.

WALKER FULLER & C? PUBLISHERS BOSTON

ABRAHAM LINCOLN

Advertisement for two publications about Abraham Lincoln: *The Pioneer Boy* and *The President's Words.* Lithograph by J. Mayer & Co., c. 1865. Prints and Photographs Division, LC-USZ62-133903

BOX 808022   PETALUMA   CA 94975

Pomegranate

Abraham Lincoln

President Lincoln delivering his second inaugural address on the east portico of the Capitol, March 4, 1865. In the audience that day was future presidential assassin John Wilkes Booth. Photograph by Alexander Gardner. Prints and Photographs Division, LC-USA7-16837

BOX 808022   PETALUMA   CA 94975

Pomegranate

ABRAHAM LINCOLN

The Peacemakers. Meeting of President Lincoln, Generals Grant and
Sherman, and Admiral Porter aboard the *River Queen* off City Point,
Virginia, March 1865. Photoprint of a painting by George P. A. Healy, 1868.
Prints and Photographs Division, LC-USZ62-67405

BOX 808022   PETALUMA   CA 94975

Pomegranate

ABRAHAM LINCOLN

Abraham Lincoln's Last Reception. Hand-colored lithograph, created
by Anton Hohenstein. Published by John Smith, 1865. Prints and
Photographs Division, LC-USZC4-2438

BOX 808022   PETALUMA   CA 94975

Pomegranate

ABRAHAM LINCOLN

Abraham Lincoln, April 10, 1865. Photograph by Alexander Gardner.
Prints and Photographs Division, LC-USZ61-1938

BOX 808022 PETALUMA CA 94975

Pomegranate

ABRAHAM LINCOLN

Abraham Lincoln. Reproduction of a painting by Howard Pyle,
created as an illustration for "Lincoln's Last Day," *Harper's Magazine,*
September 1907. General Collections

BOX 808022 PETALUMA CA 94975

Pomegranate

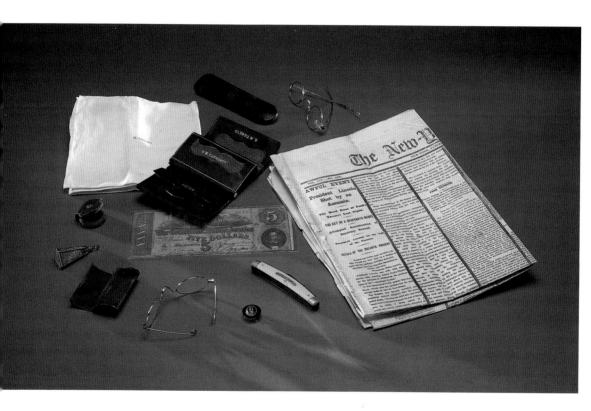

Abraham Lincoln

The contents of Abraham Lincoln's pockets on the night he was assassinated, shown with the *New York Times* edition reporting the assassination. Rare Book and Special Collections Division

Pomegranate

BOX 808022   PETALUMA   CA 94975

ABRAHAM LINCOLN

Lincoln Centennial, Grand March. E. T. Paull Music Company, 1909.
Music Division

BOX 808022   PETALUMA   CA 94975

Pomegranate